CROCODILE VS. DEINOSUCHUS

BY CHARLES C. HOFER

CAPSTONE PRESS
a capstone imprint

Published by Capstone Press, an imprint of Capstone.
1710 Roe Crest Drive, North Mankato, Minnesota 56003
capstonepub.com

Library of Congress Cataloging-in-Publication Data
Names: Hofer, Charles, author.
Title: Crocodile vs. deinosuchus / by Charles C. Hofer.
Other titles: Crocodile versus deinosuchus
Description: North Mankato, Minnesota : Capstone Press, [2024] | Series: Beastly battles | Includes bibliographical references and index. | Audience: Ages 9-11 Audience: Grades 4-6
Summary: "It's a fight between two fierce armored reptiles! Today's crocodiles are powerful, sneaky hunters. But millions of years ago, the deinosuchus was one of the biggest predators of its time. Learn what makes these similar beasts so dangerous. Then decide which of the fearsome foes would emerge victorious in a beastly brawl"— Provided by publisher.
Identifiers: LCCN 2023019026 (print) | LCCN 2023019027 (ebook) | ISBN 9781669065135 (hardcover) | ISBN 9781669065364 (paperback) | ISBN 9781669065173 (pdf) | ISBN 9781669065388 (kindle edition) | ISBN 9781669065371 (epub) Subjects: LCSH: Crocodiles—Juvenile literature. | Deinosuchus—Juvenile literature.
Classification: LCC QL666.C925 H595 2024 (print) | LCC QL666.C925 (ebook) DDC 597.98/2—dc23/eng/20230513
LC record available at https://lccn.loc.gov/2023019026
LC ebook record available at https://lccn.loc.gov/2023019027

Editorial Credits
Editor: Aaron Sautter; Designer: Bobbie Nuytten; Media Researcher: Rebekah Hubstenberger: Production Specialist: Whitney Schaefer

Image Credits
Alamy: Dorling Kindersley ltd, 29, Universal Images Group North America LLC/DeAgostini, 15; Capstone: Jon Hughes, Cover (bottom), 23, 26; Getty Images: Dorling Kindersley, 5 (bottom), iStock/Charoenchai Tothaisong, 28, iStock/hindenburgdalhoff, 21, Jeoffrey Maitem, 5 (top), Paul Starosta, 13, Tibor Bognar, 25; Newscom: Dorling Kindersley/Universal Images Group, 10-11 (middle); Science Source: John Sibbick, 7, Millard H. Sharp, 19; Shutterstock: BINK0NTAN, Cover (bottom background), 10-11 (bottom), Coral Brunner, Cover (top), 9, Nazeri Mamat, 12, Shane Bartie, 8, Vladimir Turkenich, 17, Zoe Ezzy, 27

TABLE OF CONTENTS

Words in **bold** are in the glossary.

BATTLE OF THE BEASTS!

CHOMP! It's a battle between two armored foes.

One of them is Deinosuchus. This **ancient** monster lived long ago. The other is the saltwater crocodile. It's the largest **reptile** living today.

Who would win a battle between these big-time biters?

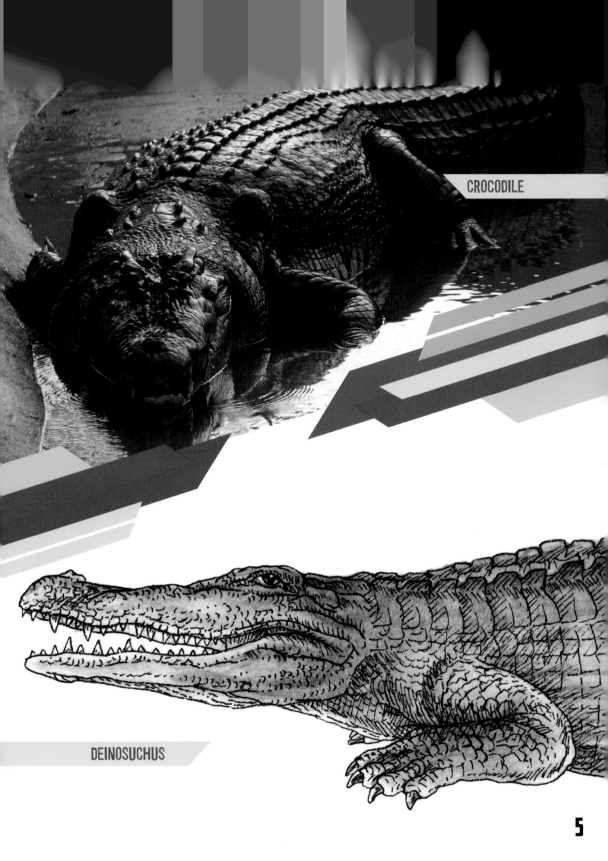

CROCODILE

DEINOSUCHUS

MEET DEINOSUCHUS

Deinosuchus was alive about 82 million years ago. It lived in what is now North America.

Deinosuchus was the largest **predator** of its time. This huge hunter lived with the dinosaurs. But no dinosaurs messed with it. Its name means "terrible crocodile."

MEET THE SALTWATER CROCODILE

Saltwater crocodiles are the largest reptiles alive today. They are found from eastern India to northern Australia. "Salties" live in rivers and lakes near the ocean.

Crocodiles are deadly predators. They eat anything they can catch. They'll eat fish, birds, small cows, or deer.

THE MEGA MONSTER

Deinosuchus was a giant. It grew to about 35-feet (10.7-meters) long. That's longer than a school bus!

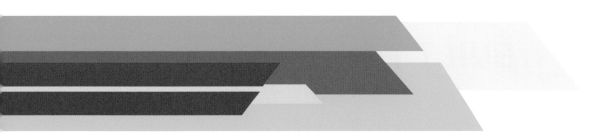

This ancient crocodile weighed about 17,000 pounds (7,700 kilograms). It's no wonder that dinosaurs kept their distance.

BUILT FOR BATTLE

The saltwater crocodile is a huge hunter. Some salties have grown up to 23-feet (7-m) long. They can weigh more than 2,000 pounds (907 kg).

The crocodile has thick skin with hard **scales**. This helps protect it from other predators.

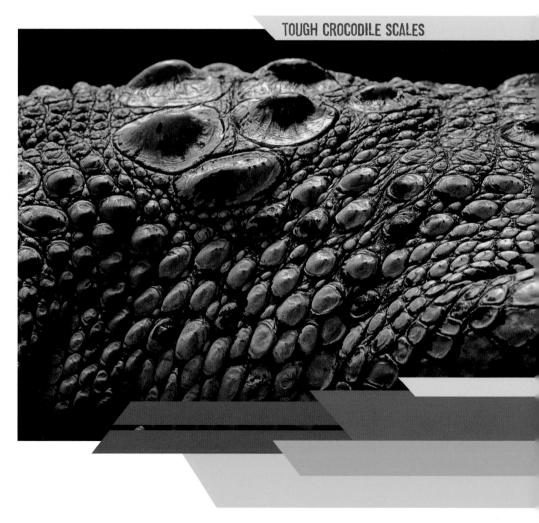

TOUGH CROCODILE SCALES

HUNGRY HUNTER

Deinosuchus had short legs. But it was quick. It could run fast on land over a short distance.

However, Deinosuchus was more at home in the water. It had a long, powerful tail. This helped it swim fast to catch **prey**.

KILLER CROC

The saltwater crocodile can run about 18 miles (29 kilometers) per hour. The fastest person in the world can run about 27 mph (43.5 kph).

But salties are faster than humans in the water. They can swim up to 18 mph (29 kph). Humans can swim only about 6 mph (10 kph). You don't want to go swimming with a saltie nearby!

BONE BREAKER

Deinosuchus had a terrible bite. Its mouth was full of sharp, jagged teeth. Its largest teeth were as big as bananas. They were up to 8 inches (20.3 centimeters) long.

Deinosuchus's skull and jaw were huge. It could crush bones with one bite. This giant croc was powerful enough to eat dinosaurs. Yum!

DEINOSUCHUS SKULL
AND TEETH

BEASTLY BITE

The saltwater crocodile's jaw is much smaller than a Deinosuchus's jaw. And its teeth are only 2.5 inches (6.4 cm) long. But it still has a powerful bite!

A saltie can have up to 68 strong teeth. They have the strongest bite of any animal alive today.

SNEAK ATTACK

Deinosuchus probably hunted in the water. This big croc liked to sneak up on prey.

The deadly hunter **stalked** animals that stood on **shore**. Then—boom! The deadly beast would burst from the water. It snatched its prey with one big bite.

CREEPING CROCODILE

The saltwater crocodile hunts from water too. Its eyes are on top of its head. It can hunt prey while it hides in the water.

These big hunters can hold their breath for up to an hour. This also helps them sneak up on prey.

BEASTLY BRAWL!

Two fearsome beasts meet in a muddy pond. One is big. But the other is huge! The saltwater croc hisses and splashes its tail. It tries to look tough.

DEINOSUCHUS

But Deinosuchus isn't scared. The mighty croc snaps its jaws. It shows off its massive teeth.

It's time for a reptile rumble!

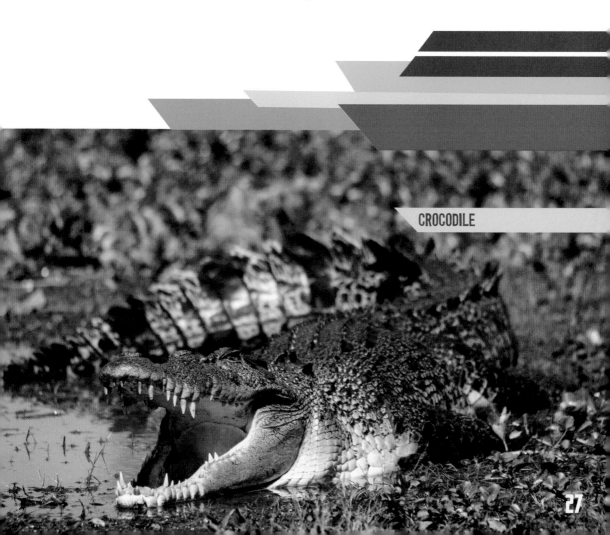

CROCODILE

WHO'S THE WINNER?

You've met the powerful foes. Deinosuchus was an ancient and terrifying beast. The saltwater crocodile rules in rivers today. Who would win between these armored enemies?

CROCODILE

	Saltwater Crocodile	Deinosuchus
HABITAT	rivers and saltwater coasts from India to Australia	swamps and rivers of North America
WEIGHT	2,000 pounds (907 kg)	17,000 pounds (7,700 kg)
LENGTH	23 feet (7m)	35 feet (10.7 m)
SPEED	runs and swims up to 18 mph (29 kph)	unknown
WEAPONS	teeth, 2.5 inches (6.4 cm) long	teeth, 8 inches (20.3 cm) long
DEFENSES	thick skin with hard scales	thick skin with hard scales
STRATEGIES	hides in water to hunt prey	hunts prey from water

DEINOSUCHUS

GLOSSARY

ancient (AYN-shunt)—from a long time ago

reptile (REP-tile)—a cold-blooded animal that breathes air and has a backbone; most reptiles have scaly skin and lay eggs

predator (PRED-uh-tur)—an animal that hunts other animals for food

prey (PRAY)—an animal that is hunted and eaten by another animal

scales (SKAYLZ)—small, hard, overlapping plates that cover the skin of reptiles and most fish

shore (SHOHR)—the place where water in an ocean, lake, or river meets land

stalk (STAWK)—to hunt an animal in a quiet, secret way

READ MORE

Emminizer, Theresa. *Saltwater Crocodile: The Largest Reptile.* New York: PowerKids Press, 2020.

Hansen, Grace. *Saltwater Crocodiles.* Minneapolis: Abdo Kids, 2019.

Rake, Matthew. *Prehistoric Sea Beasts.* Minneapolis: Hungry Tomato, 2017.

INTERNET SITES

American Museum of Natural History: Ancient Crocs
amnh.org/exhibitions/crocs/ancient-crocs

Brisbane Kids: Saltwater Crocodile Facts for Kids
brisbanekids.com.au/saltwater-crocodile-facts-for-kids

DK Find Out: Crocodiles and Alligators
dkfindout.com/us/animals-and-nature/reptiles/crocodiles-and-alligators

INDEX

ABOUT THE AUTHOR

Charles C. Hofer is a biologist and writer living in New Mexico. He hopes he never gets caught in a fight between a Deinosuchus and a saltie.